Lip Smacking
Dishes of Kerala

Cuisinart Publishers

Nimi Sunilkumar

Lip Smacking Dishes of Kerala

Published by

Cuisinart Publishers

SN Sadanam , A.M .Road, Munnar, Idukki(dt.), Kerala, India-685612.

www.ca-publishers.org

Copyright © 2013 by Cuisinart Publishers

ISBN 978-81-926491-0-8

All rights reserved. No part of this publication may be re-produced, stored in retrieval system or transmitted in any form or by any means, electronic, magnetic tape, mechanical, photo copying, recording or otherwise without prior permission of the publisher.

Author: Nimi Sunil kumar

Photography: Nimi Sunil kumar

Art Work: O.T.Remanan & Dileep

Printed in India

For Marketing & Sales inquiries : sales@ca-publishers.org

First Edition: December 2009

Second Edition: April 2013

Price: ₹ 400/-

"In the childhood memories of every good cook there's a large kitchen, a warm stove, a simmering pot and a mom."

Barbara Costikyan

My personal story is braided with this quote as my mom was always my real source of inspiration. I used to envy my mom's skill in twisting up an array of dishes in minutes. After my studies in Electronics and Communication, I was married off into a joint family where all the members enjoyed cooking. My flair for cooking sprung up in full bloom after my marriage with Sunil. For a few years, I pursued my career as a freelance writer. I really feel lucky to have a person like Sunil as my life partner who like me is a food lover. I started my food blog, "Nimi's Culinary Ventures" in 2009 in an effort to treasure my trials in my kitchen lab. In 2010, my first book on authentic food of Kerala was released in an effort to expose the taste and aroma of Kerala cuisine. In Jan 2012, I opened up my very own "Lip Smacking Cooking Classes" in Munnar, teaching traditional Kerala cooking to travellers.

This book is an effort to bring mouth-watering delicacies of Kerala homes in its very own authentic way. My special thanks go to my parents, in laws, my brother, family members and all those who have shared their recipes. Thanks to O.T.Remanan and Dileep for giving a radiant breath of colours through their art work.

For more recipes log on to **www.nimisrecipes.com**

Wishing all a lip smacking cooking!

nimi@nimisrecipes.com

Contents

1. Puttu 07
2. Paalappam 09
3. Idiyappam 11
4. Ari Pathiri 13
5. Uppuma 15
6. Idli 17
7. Kappa Kuzhachathu 19
8. Thattilkutty dosa 21
9. Pidi 23
10. Kadala curry 25
11. Vegetable Stew 27
12. Mutton stew 29
13. Mutta Roast 31
14. Thenga chammanthi 33
15. Sambar 35
16. Aviyal 37
17. Achinga thoran 39
18. Pulisseri 41
19. Parippu curry 43
20. Kurukku kalan 45
21. Mambazha pulisseri 47
22. Pineapple pachadi 49
23. Mathanga Payar erissery 51
24. Olan 53
25. Vellarikka Pachadi 55
26. Beetroot Pachadi 57
27. Manga chammanthi 59
28. Unakka chemmeen chammanthi 61
29. Vazhachundu payar thoran 63
30. Idichakka thoran 65
31. Chakka puzhukku 67
32. Meen Varuthathu 69
33. Karimeen Pollichathu 71
34. Chemmeen Roast 73
35. Meen mulagittathu 75
36. Thenga arachameen curry 77
37. Chemmeen muringakol theeyal 79
38. Meen Peera 81
39. Naadan koonthal curry 83
40. Naadan kozhi curry 85
41. Varutharacha kozhi curry 87
42. Mutton Ularthiyathu 89
43. Beef Vindaloo 91
44. Njandu Roast 93
45. Ney choru 95
46. Meen Biriyani 97
47. Thalassery Biriyani 99
48. Parippuvada 101
49. Unniyappam 103
50. Pazhampori 105
51. Unnakkayi 107
52. Vattayappam 109
53. Kinnathappam 111
54. Kozhiada 113
55. Kozhukatta 115
56. Inji curry 117
57. Irumban Puli achar 119
58. Paal Ada Prathaman 121
59. Ada prathaman 123
60. Thulsi Wine 125
61. Tips for keralan touch 127

This book is a special dedication to the three musketeers in my life - my husband Sunilkumar and my sons, Surjeeth & Sivasankar.

Puttu
Steamed rice cake

Ingredients

2 cups of Puttu Powder (Coarse rice flour)
1 cup of Scraped coconut
½ tsp. cumin seeds
Water as required
Salt to taste

Method of preparation:

In a bowl add cumin seeds to the Puttu powder.

Take required amount of water(about 2/3 of a cup) adding salt to taste it.

Sprinkle and mix the water into the puttu powder.Take care not to pour the water all at once.

It should become like bread crumbs and not dough.Mix evenly.

Puttu is to be made in a puttu maker.Take the puttukutti (cylindrical piece of the puttu maker)with its sieve in and fill it with a handful of scraped coconut and then add the rice flour mix till it reaches about half of the cylinder.Now layer it with scraped coconut,rice flour and again with scraped coconut at the top and close the lid.

Boil water in the puttukudam (pot) and place the puttukutti (the cylindrical part with the sieve disc in it) on top of it.

Steam for about 10 minutes on medium flame.

Puttu is best served with kadalacurry /ripe bananas.

Paalappam

Lotus pancakes

Ingredients

¼ kg Raw rice
3 tbsps of cooked rice
1tsp of yeast granules dissolved in 1-2 tbsp of hot water
1tbsp sugar
Salt to taste

For grinding

½ cup scraped coconut
½ tsp cumin seeds
½ cup of shallots
2 cloves of garlic

Method of preparation:

Wash and soak the raw rice for 4-5 hrs in water.

Once soaked, add cooked rice with it and grind it into a smooth paste by adding water and keep aside.

In a saucepan pour ¼ of the batter and 2 cups of plain water. Stir and cook the mixture on medium heat to make porridge.

Let the porridge cool down a bit and mix in the yeast. Now mix this to the rice batter thoroughly, cover and keep it overnight for fermentation.

Once the batter has been fermented, grind coconut, cumin, shallots & garlic to make a coarse mix. Mix the crushed mix with salt and sugar into the batter and keep it for about 20 minutes.

Paalappams are normally made in Appachattis made of iron or non stick. If using iron appachattis, smear oil in pan before making the appams.

Heat the appachatti, pour 1 ½ ladle of batter in the center of the pan and swirl the pan to get a thin layer of the batter covering the sides and a thick layer at the center of the pan.

Cover with a lid and cook the appams till the sides are golden brown and the edges come off the pan easily.

These fluffy pancakes are one of Kerala's most renown delicacies. They are a great combination with vegetable stew/mutton stew/ kadala curry/egg roast.

Idiyappam
Steamed String hoppers

Ingredients

2 cups of rice flour
1 cup of scraped coconut
3 cups of water
2 tsp sugar
¼ tsp cumin seeds
1 tbsp of coconut oil
Salt to taste

Method of preparation:

Boil water with salt to taste in a pan. When the water starts boiling, add in coconut oil and lower the heat to medium flame.

Add in the rice flour stirring constantly with a ladle so that it is evenly kneaded into dough. Turn off the flame and set it aside for cooling.

In a small bowl mix coconut, sugar and cumin seeds and keep it aside.

The idiyappams are steamed in an idli steamer. Grease the idli plates with coconut oil.

Spoon in ¼ of a tsp of the coconut mix into each depression of the idli plates.

Knead the rice dough and make cylinders out of the dough.

The idiyappams are squeezed out through an idiyappam presser.

Insert the small holed sieve into the idiyappam presser and fill it with the rice cylinders .Screw on the upper part of the presser and squeeze them out in strings on to the depressions of the idli plate.

Steam the idiyappams for about 10 -15 minutes on medium flame.

Idiyappams are great to be served with Egg curries /Kadala curry / Sweetened coconut milk.

Ari pathiri
Rice roti

Ingredients

2 cups of rice flour
2 cups of water
Salt to taste
1 cup of thick coconut milk

Method of preparation:

Boil water, add salt and stir in the rice flour using a spatula to make into crumbled texture.

Transfer this on to a plate. Take about 1 cup of water in a bowl, wet your hands and knead the dough. Continue the same pattern of wetting hands and knead the dough to make a soft dough.

Make the dough into small balls and dust them with rice flour. Dust them and roll them out into thin discs.

Heat a flat frying pan or tawa and cook both sides of the pathiri. These pathiris are tastier when they are soaked in coconut milk while eating.

The best combination for pathiri is chicken curry.

Uppuma
Semolina stir fry

Ingredients

2 cups of Semolina
1 tbsp ghee
¼ cup Coconut oil
3-4 greenchillies chopped
2 large onions chopped
1 tsp ginger chopped
4 ½ cups of water
2 Dry red chillies (broken into pieces)
1 tsp mustard seeds
½ tsp black gram split /urad dal
Curry leaves
Salt to taste

Method of preparation:

In a pan on medium flame, slightly fry the semolina in ghee. Take care that the color doesn't change and remove from flame and keep it aside.

Heatoil in a pan, splutter mustard seeds, black gram split, dry red chillies and sauté green chillies, onions, ginger till the onions are translucent.

Lower the flame and pour the measured water in the pan. Once the water starts simmering, stir inthe required amount of salt.

Add the fried semolina in batches stirring continuously. To avoid the formation of lumps. Cover with a lid and remove from flame.

Uppuma is best served with bananas.

Idli
Steamed rice cakes

Ingredients

4 cups of Idli rice
1 cup of black lentils (de skinned)/urad dal
¼ tsp of fenugreek
Salt to taste

Method of preparation:

Wash and soak the idli rice and black lentils along with fenugreek for about 6-8 hours in two different bowls separately.

Once soaked, grind the black lentils and fenugreek until smooth and fluffy in a wet grinder adding the required amount of water to grind. Take care not to add too much of water. Once ground, separate the batter into a bowl. Now similarly grind the idli rice smoothly adding the adequate amount of water.

Separate it into the same bowl with the ground urad dal. Add salt to taste and mix well. Cover and keep it for fermentation overnight.

Next day morning mix the fermented batter well with a ladle and add salt if less.

Idlis are normally steamed in an idli steamer. Heat water in the steamer. The depressions in the idli plates should be greased with coconut oil and the idli batter is poured into each of the depressions and covered and steamed in the steamer for about 15 minutes.

Idlis are best served with sambar and coconut chutny.

Kappa kuzhachathu
Tapioca mix

Ingredients

½ kg tapioca cleaned and roughly chopped into cubes
Salt to taste

For grinding

1 tsp Cumin seeds
½ tsp turmeric powder
½ cup scraped coconut
4 cloves of garlic
3 shallots
4 green chillies

For seasoning

2 tsp of Coconut oil
1 tsp Mustard seeds
5 shallots Sliced
Curry leaves

Method of preparation:

Cook the tapioca pieces in salted water and sieve out.

Grind the cumin, turmeric powder, coconut, garlic, green chillies and shallots coarsely.

Mash the tapioca in a heavy bottomed pan and mix in the ground coconut on medium flame for about 3 -4 minutes and then turn off the flame.

In a small pan for seasoning, heat oil, pop mustard seeds, add in curry leaves and fry the shallots till they are golden brown.

Mix the seasoning well in to the cooked tapioca mix.

Kappa kuzhachathu is best served with fish curry and rice.

Thattilkuttydosa
Mini pancakes

Ingredients

1 ¼ cup of Black lentils (deskinned)
½ cup of raw rice
1 ½ cup of Idli rice
1/8 cup of cooked rice
Salt to taste
Ghee for frying

Method of preparation:

Wash and soak lentils, raw rice and idli rice in different bowls for about 5-6 hours.

Grind the lentils with cooked rice and required amount of water in to a fine pasteand set aside in a bowl. Grind the raw rice and idli rice to a smooth paste and mix it with the urad dal paste.

Mix the batter with the required amount of salt in a big vessel, cover and keep for fermentation for 5-6 hours.

After fermentation, mix the batter well, stir in the required amount of water to get a batter of dropping consistency.

Heat a flat frying pan or dosa tawa slightly grease with ghee, pour 1 ladle of the batter in the centre and let it cook for medium flame making small dosas. Slightly drizzle ghee on the sides of the dosa. Flip it over, cook the other side till golden and take it on to a plate when soft. Take care not to dry out the dosas.

These dosas are best served with coconut chutney and sambar.

Pidi
Rice dumplings

Ingredients

2 cups of rice flour
1 cup of scraped coconut
½ tsp cumin seeds
100g roasted and powdered par boiled rice
Salt to taste

Method of preparation:

Make dough mixing rice flour, scraped coconut, cumin seeds and salt with hot water.

Make small gooseberry sized balls of even size out of the dough. Sprinkle a little rice flour on the balls so that they don't stick together.

In a wok, pour 4 cups of water and bring it to boil. Drop in the small balls in to the water and let it boil for about 4-5 minutes.

Add powdered parboiled rice in it and on thickening remove from flame.

The best combination with Pidi would be Chicken curry.

Kadala curry
Chickpeas in fried coconut gravy

Ingredients

1 cup of Black chickpeas/chana (soaked overnight)
2 large onions (chopped)
3 Green chillies (julienne)
1 medium sized tomato (chopped)
½ tsp of Turmeric powder
1 tsp of Kashmiri chilli powder
2 tsp of Coriander powder
1 tsp of Garam masala powder
½ tsp of Mustard seeds
Curry leaves
Salt to taste

For grinding
1 tsp of oil
1 cup scraped coconut
4 shallots
4 cloves of garlic
3 Dry red chillies (broken into pieces)
½ tsp of Black pepper

Method of preparation:

In a pan pour 1 tbsp of oil and fry the items for grinding till it turns golden brown. Grind it in to a smooth paste.

Pressure cook the chickpeas with salt and green chillies.

In a heavy bottomed pan pour 2 tbsp of oil and splutter mustard seeds, dry red chillies, curry leaves and add the onions sautéing them till they are translucent.

Add chillipowder, coriander powder, garam masala powder, tomato and ½ cup water, cover and cook the tomato on medium flame.

Add in the cooked chickpeas and coconut paste adding water to get a gravy. Let it simmer and when the gravy thickens remove from flame.

Kadala Curry is best served with puttu / Idiyappams / Appams.

Vegetable Stew
Vegetables cooked in Coconut milk

Ingredients

2 potatoes diced
2 carrots diced
½ cup of green peas
5-6 beans diced
1 large onion sliced
4-5 green chillies julienned
3 cloves
3 cardamoms
1 piece of cinnamon stick
1 tsp of black peppercorns crushed
1 ½ cup thin coconut Milk
½ cup of thick coconut milk
2 tsp of oil
Coriander leaves
Curry leaves
Salt to taste

Method of preparation:

Heat oil in a pan and fry cloves, cardamoms, cinnamon and black pepper. Sauté the large onions till they are translucent with the green chillies. Add in the vegetables and stir in the thin coconut milk with the required amount of salt.

Cover the pan with a lid and cook the vegetables. When the vegetables are cooked add in the thick coconut milk, let the gravy thicken and remove from flame. Garnish with freshly chopped coriander leaves and a few curry leaves.

Vegetable stew is a good combination for Paalappams /Idiyappams.

Mutton Stew

Mutton cooked in coconut milk

Ingredients

½ kg Mutton cleaned and cut in to cubes
2 medium sized potatoes cubed
2 large onions sliced
6 green chillies julienned
¼ cup of All purpose flour
3 Cardamoms
4 cloves
1 -2 small sticks of Cinnamon broken in to pieces
1 piece of ginger crushed
4 -5 cloves of garlic crushed
2 tsp of Black peppercorns crushed
1 cup Thick coconut milk
½ cup thin coconut milk
3 tbsp of oil
Curry leaves
Coriander leaves
Salt to taste

Method of preparation:

Heat 3 tbsp of oil in a pressure cooker. Fry and separate the cardamom, cloves, cinnamon, black pepper, green chillies, ginger, garlic and large onions.

In the remaining oil on low flame add the all purpose flour and stir. Add the mutton pieces along with the fried items and salt, mixing well. Add thin coconut milk, stir, and cover with the lid and pressure-cook the mutton till the meat is tender.

Now add in the thick coconut milk and let the gravy thicken.

Add curry leaves, coriander leaves and remove from flame.

Mutton stew is best served with Paalappams.

Mutta Roast
Egg roast

Ingredients

3 hardboiled eggs
4 green chillies julienned
1 inch small piece of ginger
4 cloves of garlic
½ tsp mustard seeds
1 tbsp Kashmiri chilly powder
2 tsp of Coriander powder
1 tsp of Garam masala powder
½ tsp turmeric powder
1 tsp Fennel seeds
4 Large onions sliced thinly
1 tomato sliced
1 cup of Thick Coconut milk
Curry leaves
Salt to taste

Method of preparation:

Pound ginger, garlic and fennel in a mortar and pestle and keep aside.

Heat 3 tbsp of oil in a wok and splutter mustard seeds. Add in the Pound mix, curry leaves, sliced onions and sauté them till the onions are transparent in colour. Add in the tomato and sauté for a few minutes.

Add in turmeric powder, chilly powder, coriander powder, garam masala powder and ¼ cup water and stir till it starts thickening.

Now add in the coconut milk and let the curry thicken.

You can make the curry quite dry by evaporating the coconut milk and makie it a point to keep on stirring. Oil can be drizzled on the sides of the pan while stirring to avoid sticking. Add in the eggs and mix in with the curry.

Mutta roast goes hand in hand with Idiyappams/ Paalappams.

Thenga Chammanthi
Coconut chutney

Ingredients

1 cup of scraped coconut
2-3 shallots
1 small piece of ginger
4 green chillies
4-5 curry leaves
Salt to taste

For seasoning

2 tsp of oil
½ tsp of mustard seeds
1 tsp of split black lentils/urad dal
2 dry red chillies broken into pieces
2 shallots sliced thinly
Curry leaves

Method of preparation:

Grind coconut, green chillies, ginger, shallots, curry leaves into a fine paste adding water and salt.

Season the chutney by heating oil in a pan, crackling mustard seeds, sauté urad dal, dry red chillies, curry leaves and pour over the chutney.

This is a breakfast coconut chutney and is best served with idlis or dosas.

Sambar
Vegetables cooked in Lentils

Ingredients

1 cup of Yellow split peas
½ tsp of turmeric powder
2 tsp of Kashmiri chilly powder
3 tbsp of Sambar powder
¼ tsp of Asafoetida powder
1 large onion chopped
1 tomato chopped
2 green chillies julienned
A small ball of tamarind soaked in ¼ cup of water
¼ kg vegetables diced into medium sized pieces (Brinjal, potato, carrot, drumsticks, pumpkin)
2 tbsp of oil
1 tsp mustard seeds
1 tsp of split black lentils/urad dal
2-3 dry red chillies torn into pieces
1 tsp of ginger finely chopped
2 tbsp of jaggery syrup
Curry leaves
Coriander leaves
Salt to taste

Method of preparation:

Wash and cook the lentils in 3 cups of water with the required amount of salt. Heat oil in pan, pop mustard, split black lentils, dry red chillies, green chillies, ginger and curry leaves. Sauté the onions, tomatoes and add in the Kashmiri chilli powder, sambar powder and turmeric powder and fry. Sieve and pour the tamarind water into this and let it simmer.

Add asafoetida powder to this and mix in the vegetables .Add this to the half cooked lentils and cook the vegetables along with lentils with the required amount of salt.

Add water if the consistency of curry is too thick. On simmering stir in the jaggery syrup and garnish with chopped coriander leaves and turn off the flame.

Sambar is an indispensable curry in Kerala. It is best served with rice /dosa/idlis.

Aviyal
Mixed Vegetable Stir fry

Ingredients

2 Potatoes
2 Carrots
2 drumsticks
2 Raw plantains
½ part of a medium sized Snake gourd
½ tsp of turmeric powder
½ tsp of Kashmirichilli powder
¼ cup Curd
1 tbsp of Coconut oil
Curry leaves
Salt to taste

For grinding:

½ tsp of cumin seeds
5- 6 green chillies
½ cup of scraped coconut
4 shallots

Method of preparation:

Clean and julienne cut all the vegetables evenly.

Marinate the vegetables with turmeric powder, Kashmiri chilly powder, salt and ½ tsp of coconut oil.

Grind the ingredients listed for grinding coarsely

Once the vegetables are cooked, add in the ground coconut mix and stir in the curd cooking on low flame.

Garnish with 1 tbsp of Coconut oil and curry leaves and turn off the flame.

Aviyal is best served with rice.

Achinga thoran
Asparagus beans stir fry

Ingredients

2 cups of asparagus beans /yard long beans cleaned and finely chopped
2 tsp of oil
½ tsp of mustard seeds
½ tsp of split black gram lentils(without skin)/urad dal
Salt to taste
Curry leaves

For grinding

¾ cup of scraped coconut
½ tsp of cumin seeds
4 cloves of garlic
5 green chillies
3-4 shallots

Method of preparation:

Grind coconut, cumin, garlic, shallots and green chillies into a coarse paste.

Heat oil in pan, splutter mustard seeds, split black gram lentils, curry leaves and sauté the coconut mix on low flame. Now add in the chopped asparagus beans, cover and cook.

Make sure to stir the beans in between so that it doesn't stick to the bottom of the pan.

Once the beans are cooked, turn off the flame.

Achinga payar thoran is best served with rice.

Pulisseri

Yoghurt curry

Ingredients

4 cup Yoghurt (whisked)
Salt to taste

For grinding:
1 cup of scraped coconut
½ tsp cumin seeds
¼ tsp turmeric powder
4 green chillies
2 cloves garlic

For seasoning
1 tbsp Coconut oil
¼ tsp mustard seeds
2 -3 dry red chillies broken into pieces
¼ tsp fenugreek
A pinch of kashmiri chilly powder
Curry leaves

Method of preparation:

Grind the ingredients for grinding into a smooth paste.

In a wok, heat oil and pop mustard seeds. To this add in the fenugreek seeds, dry red chillies, pinch of chilly powder, curry leaves and stir.

Add in the coconut paste and pour in the yogurt and stir on low flame.

When steam starts rising from the curry turn it off.

Pulisseri is best served with rice.

Parippu curry
Green gram split in coconut gravy

Ingredients

1 cup Green gram split lentils/Moong dal
½ tsp of turmeric powder
Salt to taste

For grinding

½ cup of scraped coconut
½ tsp of cumin
4 green chillies
4 cloves of garlic
½ tsp of turmeric powder
2-3 shallots

For seasoning

1 tbsp of oil
1 tsp of mustard seeds
3 -4 shallots sliced
2-3 dry red chillies broken into pieces
Curry leaves

Method of preparation:

Grind the items for grinding into a smooth paste.

Wash and pressure cook the lentils with turmeric powder and salt in water.

Once cooked, add in the coconut paste and stir. Add water if the curry is too thick in consistency and let it simmer for a few minutes.

Heat oil in a pan, splutter mustard seeds, add dry red chillies, curry leaves and sauté the shallots till golden brown and pour over the curry.

Parippu curry is best served with rice.

Kurukku Kalan

Vegetables cooked in curd

Ingredients

½ cup of raw plantains diced into small pieces
½ cup of yam diced in to small pieces
½ tsp of turmeric powder
3 cups of curd , whisked
Salt to taste

For grinding

1 cup of scraped coconut
4 green chillies
½ tsp of cumin seeds
¼ tsp of turmeric powder
5-6 peppercorns

For seasoning

2 tsp of oil
1 tsp mustard seeds
½ tsp fenugreek seeds
3 dry red chillies (broken in to pieces)
Curry leaves

Method of preparation:

Rinse and drain the plantain pieces in warm turmeric powder to remove the starchy content.

In a heavy bottomed vessel, cook plantain and yam pieces in 2 cups of water with turmeric powder and salt.

Grind the ingredients for grinding in to a smooth paste.

Once the vegetables are cooked, add in the ground coconut paste to it and let it simmer. Slowly stir in the curd so that it mixes well with the vegetables and coconut paste.

Keep stirring on medium flame till the curry gets thick.

Season the curry by heating oil in a pan, spluttering mustard seeds, fenugreek seeds, dry red chillies, curry leaves and pour over the curry.

Kurukku kalan is best served with rice. It is one among the famous side dishes for Sadhya.

Mambazha pulisseri
Ripe mangoes cooked in curd

Ingredients

½ kg of small ripe mangoes
1 tsp of Kashmiri chilly powder
½ tsp of turmeric powder
2 cups of curd
1 tbsp of jaggery syrup or sugar
2 tsp of oil
1/2 tsp of mustard seeds
½ tsp of fenugreek
3 dry red chillies, broken into pieces
Curry leaves
Salt to taste

For grinding

1 cup of scraped coconut
1 tsp of cumin
½ tsp of black peppercorns
½ tsp of turmeric powder
4-5 green chillies
2 shallots
3 cloves of garlic

Method of preparation:

Cook the ripe mangoes with turmeric powder, chilli powder and salt in about ½ cup of water.

Grind the items listed for grinding into a smooth paste.

Add this to the cooked mangoes and let it simmer.

Whisk the curd and stir this into the mangoes and heat it for a few minutes and turn off the flame.

Heat oil in a pan, pop mustard seeds, sauté fenugreek seeds, dry chillies and curry leaves .Pour the seasoning over the curry.

Mambazha pulisseri is best served with rice.

Pineapple pachadi

Pineapple cooked with coconut and curd

Ingredients

1 medium sized ripe pineapple, cleaned and chopped
2 tsp of oil
½ tsp of turmeric powder
1 tbsp of jaggery syrup or 2 tsp of sugar
1 tsp of mustard seeds
2-3 dry red chillies, broken into pieces
1 cup of curd
Curry leaves
Salt to taste

For grinding

½ tsp of turmeric powder
1 cup of scraped or grated coconut
½ tsp of mustard seeds
5-6 green chillies
½ tsp of cumin
2-3 shallots
2 cloves of garlic

Method of preparation:

Cook the pineapple pieces in ½ cup of water with turmeric powder and salt till soft.

Grind all the items for grinding into a smooth paste in a mixer.

Mix in the ground paste to the pineapple pieces, add ¼ cup of water and let it simmer for 10 minutes.

Whisk the curd and stir it into the pineapple coconut mix. Add sugar or jaggery syrup .You can add more sweetness depending on your taste. Heat it for a few minutes on medium flame and set aside.

Pineapple pachadi is a variation of the Mathura curries/sweet curries and is best served with rice.

Season the curry by heating oil in a pan, splutter mustard seeds, sauté dry red chillies and curry leaves and pour it over the pineapple pachadi.

Mathanga Payar Erissery
Pumpkin & red beans curry

Ingredients

¼ kg pumpkin deseeded and cut in to cubes
½ tsp of turmeric powder
½ tsp of chilli powder
100g Dry red beans, soaked overnight
Salt to taste

For grinding

½ cup of scraped coconut
3 cloves of garlic
2 shallots
¼ tsp of cumin seeds
½ tsp of chilli powder
¼ tsp of turmeric powder

For seasoning

3 tsp of coconut oil
1 tsp of mustard seeds
1 tsp of split black gram lentils/urad dal
2-3 dry red chillies broken into pieces
½ cup of scraped coconut
Curry leaves

Method of preparation:

Cook dry red beans in water with salt and when they are half cooked add in the pumpkins with chilli powder and turmeric powder and cook till they are soft by adding water. In the meanwhile make a coarse paste of the ingredients that are to be ground.

Heat a pan, pour oil, pop mustard seeds, urad dal, dry red chilies, curry leaves and add in the coconut and fry till it becomes golden brown in color and set aside.

Add in the ground coconut mix with the pumpkin and dry red beans on medium flame and stir.

Season this with the fried coconut mix and mix well.

Mathanga payar erissery is best served with rice.

Olan
Ash gourd and dry red beans in coconut milk

Ingredients

1 medium sized Ash gourd (peeled, deseeded & cut into thin slices)
¼ cup Dry red beans
1 cup thick Coconut milk
6 Green chillies (julienned)
3 Tbsp of Coconut oil
Curry leaves
Salt to taste

Method of preparation:

Cook the ash gourd pieces with green chillies and salt in water

Cook the dry red beans with salt separately in water and strain

Mix the dry red beans with the Ash gourd on low flame. Pour in the thick coconut milk.

When it starts to simmer, mix in fresh curry leaves and coconut oil and turn down the flame.

Olan is best served with rice.

Vellarika Pachadi
Yellow skinned cucumber in coconut & curd gravy

Ingredients

1 cup of yellow skinned cucumber peeled and chopped
5 green chillies julienned
1 cup curd
Salt to taste

For grinding

1 cup of scraped coconut
4 shallots
2-3 cloves of garlic
½ tsp of mustard seeds

For seasoning

2 tsp of oil
½ tsp of mustard seeds
¼ tsp of fenugreek seeds
2 dry red chillies(broken into pieces)
Curry leaves

Method of preparation:

Grind the coconut, shallots, garlic and mustard seeds in to a smooth paste.

Cook cucumber with salt and green chillies in water.

Once the cucumber is cooked turn the flame low and add in the coconut paste. Stir in the curd and turn off the flame.

In a small pan heat oil ,pop mustard seeds, fenugreek ,dry red chillies and curry leaves and mix this seasoning into the gravy.

Vellarikka pachadi is best served with rice.

Beetroot Pachadi
Beetroot in coconut gravy

Ingredients

2 medium sized beetroots(finely chopped/grated)
5 green chillies, chopped
1 cup curd
Salt to taste

For grinding

1 cup of scraped coconut
2 cloves of garlic
1/2 tsp of mustard seeds

For seasoning

3 tsp of oil
½ tsp mustard seeds
2 dry redchillies (broken)
¼ tsp fenugreek seeds
Curry leaves

Method of preparation:

Grind the items for the coconut paste into a smooth paste and keep it aside.

Cook the beetroot with green chillies and salt in ½ cup of water .Mix in the coconut paste and keeping it on low flame, stir in the curd.

Heat oil in a small pan and season the curry with mustard seeds, fenugreek seeds,dry red chillies and curry leaves. Beetroot Pachadi is best served with rice.

Manga Chammanthi
Mango chutney

Ingredients

5 pieces of Green mango
4 green chillies
½ cup of scraped coconut
A small piece of ginger
2 shallots
Curry leaves (4-5)
Salt to taste

Method of preparation:

In a mixer bowl grind all the ingredients together by adding very little water with the required amount of salt.

Once ground, mix in a teaspoon of coconut oil.

This chutney is best served with rice.

Unakka Chemmeen chammanthi
Dried shrimps chutney

Ingredients

1 cup of dried shrimps, cleaned (head and tail taken off)
1 cup of scraped coconut
5 -6 dry red chillies
A small piece of ginger
4 cloves of garlic
2 shallots
A small piece of tamarind
Salt to taste

Method of preparation:

Wash the shrimps in water and drain them.

Dry roast them in a small skillet on low flame. Add in all the other ingredients except salt and slightly fry them for a few minutes and let it cool down a bit.

Grind the roasted mix in a mixer jar coarsely with salt to taste.

Unakka chemmeen chammanthi is best served with rice.

Vazhachundu payar thoran
Banana flower and green gram stir fry

Ingredients

1 cup of Banana flower chopped
1 cup of Greengram soaked overnight
2tsp of oil
½ tsp of Mustard seeds
Curry leaves
Salt to taste

For grinding

1 cup of Scraped coconut
½ tsp of cumin
½ tsp of turmeric powder
5 shallots
3 cloves of garlic

Method of preparation:

Cook the green gram and banana flower together with salt and water. Grind the shallots, coconut, cumin, turmeric powder, shallots and garlic into a coarse mix.

Heat oil in a pan and splutter mustard seeds. Sauté the coconut mix with curry leaves for a few minutes and mix in the cooked banana flower, greengram and turn off the heat.

Vazhachundu payar thoran is best served with rice.

Idichakka Thoran
Tender jackfruit stir-fry

Ingredients

1 small tender jackfruit
1 tsp of mustard seeds
1 tsp of split black lentils
2-3 dry red chillies, broken in to pieces
1 tsp of oil
Curry leaves

For the coconut mix
1 cup of scraped coconut
2-3 shallots
3 cloves of garlic
5 green chillies
½ tsp of cumin

Method of preparation:

Grind the ingredients for the coconut mix coarsely in a mixer and keep aside.

Cut of the skin of the tender jackfruit, cut first into 2 halves then cut them into 4 halves. Slice of the hard core of the pieces and chop them into small pieces.

Pressure-cook them with ½ tsp of turmeric powder and salt to taste. Once cooked, pound these pieces in a mortar and pestle so that they shred into pieces.

Heat oil in a wok, pop mustard seeds with split black lentils dry red chillies and curry leaves.

Add in the coconut mix and fry for few minutes. Mix in the cooked and pound jackfruit pieces well with the coconut, stir fry for two minutes and turn off the flame.

Idichakka thoran is best served with rice as a stir-fry.

Chakka Puzhukku
Mashed Jackfruit with coconut

Ingredients

2 cups of unripe jackfruit bulbs deseeded & chopped
½ tsp turmeric powder
Salt to taste

For grinding

½ cup of scraped coconut
½ tsp cumin
4-5 black peppercons
2-3 shallots
4 green chillies
2 cloves of garlic

For seasoning

2-3 finely sliced shallots
1-2 tsp of coconut oil
1 tsp mustard seeds
Curry leaves

Method of preparation:

Cook the jackfruit pieces with turmeric powder and salt till they are soft.

Grind all the ingredients coarsely and add to the soft jack fruit pieces on low flame.

Mix the coconut paste well into the jack fruit pieces.

In small pan pour oil, splutter mustard seeds, sauté sliced shallots till golden add curry leaves & season the mashed jackfruit mix.

Chakka puzhukku can be served with mango pickle / fish curry.

Meen varuthathu
Fish fry

Ingredients

½ kg fish
Oil for frying

For marinating
3tbsp of Kashmiri chilli powder
½tsp of turmeric powder
1tsp of ginger and garlic paste
2 shallots
1tbsp of black pepper powder
½tsp of coriander powder
Salt to taste

Method of preparation:

Grind all the ingredients for marinating into a smooth paste in a mixer bowl.

Marinate the fish pieces and keep them aside for about half an hour.

Heat oil in a frying pan and slide in the fish pieces. Fry both sides of the fish till they are brown on both sides and separate.

Karimeen pollichathu
Pearl spot fish fried in banana leaf

Ingredients

1 medium sized pearl spot fish cleaned
2 tbsp of coconut oil
½ cup of shallots sliced
3-4 green chillies
1 small piece of ginger
4 clove of garlic
½ cup of thick coconut milk
1 banana leaf

For marinating

½ tsp turmeric powder
2 tsp of Kashmiri chilly powder
1 tsp of black pepper powder
½ tsp of garam masala powder
½ tsp of vinegar
Salt to taste

Method of preparation:

Make diagonal gashes on the cleaned pearl spot fish.

Prepare the banana leaf, by slightly tempering it over flame(hold by the tips of the leaf and move it above the fire) so that it slightly fades in colour and helps in folding. This lessens the chances of tearing the banana leaf while wrapping the fish. Keep the leaf aside.

Grind the ingredients for marinating in a mixer bowl and marinate the fish inside out.Keep the masala paste that remains after marinating the fish. Pound green chillies, ginger and garlic in a mortar and pestle.

Heat oil in a pan, stir the crushed items, sauté the shallots till translucent, add the remaining masala paste and stir.

Gently add in the marinated fish, pour ½ cup of thick coconut milk and let the gravy become thick and turn off the flame.

Take the prepared banana leaf, keep the fish with all the gravy on the fish and wrap the fish in the banana leaf and tie it with a string.

In a flat frying pan , pour 1-2tsp of coconut oil and place the wrapped fish .Cover and cook on both sides of the wrapped fish till done. Slightly drizzle oil on the sides if u feel the wrap is sticking to the pan.

Open the wrap once done(the leaf is a bit more browner) and serve with onion rings and lime.

Chemmeen Roast
Prawn roast

Ingredients

½kg prawns
2 tbsp of oil
1 cup of Shallots (crushed)
5 cloves of garlic
1 inch piece of ginger
½ tsp of Fennel seeds
3 Green chillies
3 pieces of Garcinia
3 tbsp of Coconut oil
¼ cup of Coconut chips
½ tsp of turmeric powder
1tsp of Black pepper powder
1 tsp of Kashmiri chilli powder
1 tsp of coriander powder
½ tsp of garam masala powder
Curry leaves
Salt to taste

Method of preparation:

Cook the prawns with turmeric powder, green chillies, salt and garcinia in water.

Pound ginger, garlic and fennel in a mortar and pestle.

Pound also the shallots and keep aside.

In a heavy bottomed pan, pour coconut oil and fry the coconut chips with a pinch of turmeric powder and salt till they are golden in colour.

Add in the pound ginger mix and shallots and sauté them well till translucent.

Keeping the flame low, add in the turmeric powder, Kashmiri chilli powder,coriander powder,black pepper powder and garam masala powder.

Add the cooked prawns to this and stir in with curry leaves. Fry the prawns well and remove from flame.

In a pan pour 2 tbsp of oil , fry the coconut pieces with a pinch of turmeric and salt till they turn crispy golden .Mix well with the prawns.

Meen mulagittathu
Spicy fish curry

Ingredients

½ kg of Fish pieces
2-3 tsp of coconut oil
3 pieces of Garcinia soaked in water
½ cup of Shallots (sliced)
A small piece of ginger (finely chopped)
5-6 cloves of Garlic (finely chopped)
½ tsp turmeric powder
1 tbsp of Kashmiri chilli powder
½ tsp of mustard seeds
¼ tsp of fenugreek seeds
Curry leaves
Salt to taste

Method of preparation:

In a pan pour 1 ½ cup of water and boil garcinia and keep aside.

In an earthen vessel or wok heat oil, splutter mustard seeds, fenugreek and curry leaves. Add the chopped ginger and garlic and keep stirring. Add in the sliced shallots and sauté till translucent.

Lower the flame and add chilly powder, turmeric powder and stir. Pour in the boiled syrup of garcinia with the pieces and stir. When the sauce starts to boil add the fish pieces, cover and cook fish. When the fish is cooked, take off the lid, let the gravy thicken and remove from flame.

Thenga aracha meen curry
Fish cooked in coconut paste

Ingredients

½ kg Fish pieces
3 pieces of Garcinia
5 of shallots
3-4 green chillies
1 piece of ginger
7-8 For seasoning
2 tsp of coconut oil
4-5 shallots sliced
Curry leaves cloves of garlic
½ tsp of turmeric powder
2-3 tsp of Kashmiri chilly powder
3 tsp of coriander powder
1 cup of scraped coconut
Curry leaves
Salt to taste

For seasoning
2 tsp of coconut oil
4-5 shallots sliced
Curry leaves

Method of preparation:

Cook the ripe mangoes with turmeric powder, chilli powder and salt in about ½ cup of water.

Grind the items listed for grinding into a smooth paste.

Add this to the cooked mangoes and let it simmer.

Pound ginger, garlic and green chillies and keep aside.

Marinate the fish pieces with chilly powder, turmeric powder, coriander powder, pound mix with 1 tsp of coconut oil and salt to taste. Add 1 cup of water to this and cook on medium flame.

Grind coconut into a smooth paste and once the fish is cooked, stir this in adding little water if needed depending on the consistency of the curry.

Heat oil in a small pan, sauté the shallots till golden brown in colour, add curry leaves and pour over the curry and mix in.

Thenga aracha meen curry is best served with rice.

Chemmeen Muringakol Theeyal
Prawns & Drumsticks in fried coconut gravy

Ingredients

½ kg Prawns (cleaned)
2 drumsticks (cut into 1inch length wise pieces)
3 green chillies julienned
1 tomato chopped
½ tsp turmeric powder
Salt to taste

For frying:
1 cup Scraped coconut
½ tsp turmeric powder
1 tsp Kashmiri chilli powder
2 tsp coriander powder
¼ tsp fennel seeds

For seasoning:
½ tsp Mustard seeds
7-8 shallots sliced
Curry leaves

Method of preparation:

Clean and cook the prawns with turmeric powder and salt.

In a pan pour 3tsp of oil, splutter mustard seeds, sauté shallots, green chillies and tomato till translucent. Add drumsticks, salt and ½ cup water it and cook on medium flame.

In the meanwhile, in a small wok on medium flame, fry the coconut with fennel seeds till brown and then add in the turmeric powder, chilly powder and coriander powder and turn off the flame.

When the coconut cools down grind it into a smooth paste in a mixer.

Add the ground paste into the cooked drumsticks along with the prawns and add 1 cup of water and let the gravy thicken on medium flame and then turn it off.

Chemmeen muringakol theeyal is best served with rice.

Meen Peera

Anchovy cooked in coconut mix

Ingredients

½ kg of anchovy
3 pieces of Garcinia
1 tbsp of coconut oil
Curry leaves
Salt to taste

For grinding

1 cup of scraped coconut
5 shallots
1 tsp of ginger chopped
4-5 green chillies
½ tsp of turmeric powder

Method of preparation:

Coarsely grind the coconut, green chillies and ginger with turmeric powder.

In an earthen vessel/wok mix the anchovy with the coconut mix, garcinia and salt to taste. Sprinkle about 1/8 cup of water and cover and cook on very low flame.

Keep stirring the mix in between so that it doesn't stick to the bottom of the vessel.

Once the fish is cooked, season it with by mixing in curry leaves and coconut oil and turn off the flame.

Meen Peera is best served with rice.

Naadan koonthal curry
Traditional kerala style Squid curry

Ingredients

¼ kg of squid, cleaned and cut
1/2 cup of shallots sliced
1 tbsp of oil
2 tsp of ginger and garlic paste
2 tsp of Kashmiri chilli powder
1 tsp of coriander powder
1 tsp of garam masala powder
1 tomato chopped
1 cup of thick coconut milk
½ tsp of turmeric powder
Curry leaves
Salt to taste

For seasoning

1 tsp of oil
2 shallots thinly sliced
Curry leaves

Method of preparation:

Cook the squid pieces with ½ tsp of turmeric powder, salt to taste and required amount of water.

Heat oil in a wok, fry the ginger and garlic paste, sauté the onions till translucent and fry the tomatoes till cooked.

Add in the turmeric powder, chilli powder, coriander powder and garam masala powder and fry for a few minutes.
Add the cooked squid to this and mix well. Pour in the thick coconut milk and let it simmer on medium flame till the sauce thickens and keep aside.

In small pan heat oil, pop mustard seeds, sauté shallots till golden brown, add in curry leaves and pour over the squid curry.

Naadan kozhi curry

Chicken and potatoes cooked in coconut milk

Ingredients

½ kg chicken pieces
3 potatoes diced into medium sized cubes
1 cup of Big onion sliced
8 cloves of garlic
½ inch piece of ginger
1 tsp of aniseed
1 ½ tbsp of Kashmiri chilly powder
1 ½ tbsp Coriander powder
½ tsp of Turmeric powder
1/8 tsp of black pepper powder
1 tsp of Garam masala powder
1 tsp of mustard seeds
1 tomato chopped
1 tbsp of vinegar
3 tbsp of coconut oil
3 green chillies , julienned
½ cup of thick coconut milk
2 cups of thin coconut milk
salt to taste

For seasoning

2 tsp of coconut oil
6 shallots sliced
Curry leaves

Method of preparation:

Mix coriander powder, chilly powder, black pepper powder, turmeric powder and garam masala powder adding little water to make it into a paste consistency and keep aside. Pound ginger and garlic with aniseed in a mortar and pestle.

Heat oil in a wok .Pop mustard seeds, fry in the ginger, garlic & aniseed mix with green chillies. Sauté the onions with tomato till translucent.

Add in the powder paste with vinegar and stir on low flame till the oil turns up.

Mix in the chicken and potato pieces so that it mixes well with the masala. Pour the thin coconut milk and add salt to taste. Cover and cook till the chicken tenderizes.

Once the chicken is cooked , add in the coconut milk and let it simmer till the sauce thickens.

Heat oil in a small pan ,sauté the shallots till golden brown, add curry leaves and season the chicken curry.

Varutharacha kozhi curry
Chicken cooked in coconut gravy

Ingredients

1 kg chicken pieces
1 cup of shallots
1 big piece of ginger
8 green chillies
6 cloves of garlic
1 tomato, chopped
1 tbsp of Kashmiri chilly powder
2 tbsp of coriander powder
1 tbsp of Garam masala powder
½ tsp of turmeric powder
Curry leaves
Salt to taste

For coconut paste

1 tsp of coconut oil
1 ½ cup of scraped coconut

For seasoning

1 tsp of coconut oil
3 dry red chillies, broken into pieces
Curry leaves

Method of preparation:

In a wok, pour oil and fry the scraped coconut till it turns golden brown and remove from flame. Let the fried coconut cool down and grind it into a smooth paste.

Pound ginger and garlic with green chillies and keep them aside.

Pour 3tbsp of oil in a heavy bottomed pan on flame. Add the pound items and sauté them adding the sliced shallots. When the onion turns translucent, add in the powders on low flame one by one ie. Turmeric powder, chilly powder, coriander powder, garam masala .Add in the tomato and fry for a few minutes.

Add the chicken pieces to the mix and along with salt and stir well. Add 2 cups of water, cover and cook the chicken till it is tenderized. Once the chicken is cooked, add in the coconut paste and let it simmer so that the gravy gets thickened.

Heat oil in a small pan for seasoning, pop mustard seeds, fry dry red chillies and curry leaves and pour over the curry.

Varutharacha kozhi curry goes hand in hand with rice and rotis.

Mutton Ularthiyathu
Roasted Mutton

Ingredients

1 kg mutton pieces
½ kg of shallots ,sliced
½ cup of thin coconut chips
1 inch piece of ginger
6 cloves of garlic
5 green chillies
1 tsp of Fennel seeds
1 tbsp of Kashmiri chilly powder
1 ½ tbsp of coriander powder
½ tsp of Turmeric powder
1 tsp of Black pepper powder
1 tsp of garam masala powder
2 tomatoes sliced
3-4tbsp of coconut oil
Curry leaves
Salt to taste

Method of preparation:

Pound ginger, garlic, fennel seeds and green chillies.

Rub and marinate the mutton pieces with crushed ginger mix, Kashmiri chilly powder, coriander powder, turmeric powder,black pepper powder, garam masala powder, tomatoes, curryleaves and salt to taste.

Pressure-cook the mutton with the required amount of water till the meat is tender and the water is evaporated.

In a heavy bottomed pan heat coconut oil and fry the coconut chips with a pinch of turmeric powder and salt.Now add in the sliced shallots fry till they are golden brown. Add the fried coconut chips with shallots to the mutton and mix well.

Mutton ularthiyathu is now ready to be served.

Beef vindaloo
Spicy Beef curry

Ingredients

1 kg of beef pieces, sliced in small rectangles
1 large onion finely chopped
3 tbsp of coconut oil
Curry leaves
Salt to taste

For grinding

2-3 tbsp of Kashmiri chilly powder
1 tbsp of mustard seeds
½ tsp of turmeric powder
2 tsp of garam masala powder
1 piece of ginger
6-7 cloves of garlic
½ cup of vinegar

Method of preparation:

Wash and drain out the beef pieces in a colander.

Grind all the ingredients for grinding into a paste and set aside.

Heat oil in a cooker, sauté the onions till translucent and add in the ground paste and fry for a few minutes till the oil starts separating.

Now add in the beef pieces, mix well and pressure cook with the required amount of salt till they are tender.

Once cooked, add curry leaves, let the sauce thicken and turn off the flame.

Beef vindaloo is a famous recipe with the Anglo-Indian communities of Kerala . This dish can be served with rice or rotis.

Njandu Roast

Kerala style Roasted crab

Ingredients

4-5 medium sized crabs cleaned and cut
2 tbsp of oil
2 large onions sliced
1 inch piece of ginger
7 cloves of garlic
½ tsp of fennel
2 tomatoes sliced
½ tsp of turmeric powder
2 tsps of Kashmiri chilli powder
2 tsps of coriander powder
1 tsp of black pepper powder
1 tsp of garam masala powder
Curry leaves
Salt to taste

Method of preparation:

Pressure-cook the crab for 1 whistle. The limbs of the crab should be slightly pound before pressure-cooking them. Pound ginger, garlic, fennel and set aside.

Heat oil in a wok, fry the ginger and garlic, sauté the onions till translucent. Stir in the tomatoes and fry till they are cooked.

Add in the powders: turmeric powder, chilli powder, coriander powder, garam masala powder and black pepper powder on low flame one by one. Add in the cooked crab, curry leaves, ¼ cup of water and salt to mix in with the masala.

Stirring in between, dry roast the crab so that it browns well and remove from flame.

Ney Choru
Ghee rice

Ingredients

2 cups of Basmati rice
4 cups of water
6 green chillies
3 large onions ,sliced
6 tbsp of Ghee
1 tsp of ginger ,crushed
1 tsp of cloves , crushed
1 piece of cinnamon
4-5 cardamoms
5 cloves
½ tsp black peppercorns
1 star anise
Salt to taste
Chopped coriander leaves
3 tbsp of cashews
3 tbsp of raisins

Method of preparation:

Wash and drain the rice and keep it aside.

In a deep bottomed vessel, pour ghee, fry and separate out half of the large onions till golden brown with cashews and raisins.

In the remaining ghee, fry cardamom, cloves, cinnamon , black pepper, star anise for a minute on low flame.

Add drained rice and fry for 3 minutes. Pour the required amount of water, add salt and let it boil. On medium flame cover and cook rice.

When the water gets evaporated, rice is cooked.

Turn off the flame and garnish with fried onions, cashews and raisins.

Ney choru is best served with chicken curry/ vegetable curries.

MeenBiriyani
Fish Biriyani

Ingredients

For rice
2 cups of Basmati rice
½ cup of Large onions, sliced
4 cups of boiled water
½ lemon
3 Cardamoms
4 cloves
1 piece of cinnamon
2 tbsp of Ghee
Salt to taste

For garnish
2 tbsps of Cashews
2 tbsps of raisins
¼ cup of large onions , sliced
Ghee for frying

For fish masala
½ kg of Fish pieces
2 large onions, sliced
2tsp of kashmirichilly powder
½ tsp of turmeric powder
1 inch piece of ginger
4-5 cloves of garlic
1 tsp of Garam masala powder
1 cup of Thick coconut milk
½ cup of chopped coriander leaves
¼ cup of Mint leaves
1 tomato sliced
Salt to taste

For marination of fish
1 tsp of Kasmiri chilli powder
½ tsp of turmeric powder
1 tsp of coriander powder
1 tsp of Meat masala/ Chicken masala
½ tsp of vinegar
Salt to taste

Method of preparation:

Wash and drain the rice.

In a heavy bottomed vessel, heat ghee and fry the spices. Add onions, sauté till translucent and add rice and fry for 5 minutes. Add water and once it starts boiling, add salt to taste and lime juice. Cover and cook on medium flame till the water get evaporated and the rice is cooked.

Marinate the fish pieces with the ingredients for marinating and deep fry and separate the fish pieces. (The fish pieces shouldn't be over fried).Pound the ginger and garlic and set aside.

The left over oil after the frying of the fish can be used to make the fish masala.Heat the oil,fry the pound ginger garlic mix, sauté onions and tomato. Once transparent, add in the chilli powder, turmeric powder, coriander powder and garam masala. Pour in the thick coconut milk and on simmering drop in the fish pieces. When the gravy thickens, add corlander leaves and mint leaves.

In a deep heavy bottomed vessel, layer the bottom with fish masala and top it with rice. Garnish it with roasted cashews and raisins and tightly close it with a lid. Keep it on low flame for 5-10 minutes and remove from flame.

Thalassery Biriyani
Biriyani from Thalassery

Ingredients

½ kg of Chicken pieces
2 cups of Jeerakashala rice/Khaima rice (short grained Biriyani rice)
4 cups of rice
25g of large onions sliced
25g of Ginger
25g of Garlic
2 tsps of White Poppy seeds
¼ cup of curd
2 tbsp of cashews
2 tbsp of raisins
½ cup of chopped coriander/cilantro leaves
Juice of 1 lemon
¼ cup of mint leaves
2 tsps of garam masala powder
2 tsps of rose water
A pinch of saffron strands
¼ cup oil
2 tbsp of ghee
Salt to taste

Method of preparation:

Wash and drain the rice.

Grind the greenchillies, ginger, garlic , white poppy seeds, lemon juice and curd to make a paste.

In a pan heat oil ,sauté the sliced onions till translucent , add in the coriander leaves and mint leaves and stir in the chicken pieces .Add half cup of water to this with salt to taste ,cover and cook till the meat is tenderized.
In a heavy bottomed vessel, heat oil with ghee and fry and separate the cashews and raisins till golden in colour. In the same deep fry ¼ cup of large onions sliced till golden in colour.

Add the drained rice in the oil fry for 2 minutes, add required amount of water and salt to taste. Cook the rice on medium flame.

When the rice is cooked, the water would have evaporated.

Soak the saffron strands in rose water.

In a heavy bottomed vessel, layer it with first chicken mix first and then with rice and fried cashews, raisins and onions. Sprinkle the saffron water and similarly layer the rest of the chicken and rice step by step. On medium flame, slightly heat the vessel on medium flame for about 5 minutes and remove from flame.

Parippu vada
Lentil fritters

Ingredients

1 cup of Bengal gram lentils/Chana dal
½ cup of shallots chopped
1 tbsp of ginger chopped
4 green chillies
Curry leaves finely chopped
½ tsp of Asafoetida powder
Oil for frying
Salt to taste

Method of preparation:

Soak Chana dal in water for 3 hrs. Drain the dal and coarsely grind the dal in a food processor without adding water.

Mix the ground dal with the finely chopped shallots, ginger, green chillies, curry leaves, salt and asafoetida powder.

Shape the mixture into small patties.

Heat oil in a wok.

Drop the patties into hot oil and deep fry them in oil till they turn golden brown in colour.

Unniyappam
Banana donuts

Ingredients

2 cups of rice flour
¼ kg of Jaggery, broken into pieces or ½ cup of brown sugar
1/2 cup of mashed bananas(small ones are more preferred)
½ tsp of sesame seeds
3 tsp of coconut pieces roasted in ghee
½ tsp of baking soda
Seeds of 3 cardamoms slightly pound
A pinch of salt
¼ tsp of dry ginger powder
Oil for frying

Method of preparation:

Heat jaggery pieces in a pan with ½ cup of water and let it melt down completely to make a jaggery syrup. Strain out the impurities and keep it aside.

In a bowl mix rice flour, melted jaggery, sesame seeds, cardamom, mashed bananas, baking soda, cardamom, salt and dry ginger powder with the required amount of water to get a batter of dropping consistency.

Heat oil in an Unniyappam Pan.
Once the oil is hot, pour batter into each of the depressions in the pan.

On medium flame, turn over the unniyappams with a fork so that both sides are evenly golden brown in colour and take them out.

The same procedure can be followed for the rest of the batter.

Pazhampori
Banana fritters

Ingredients

2 -3 ripe plantains
1 cup of all purpose flour
2 tbsp of rice flour
½ tsp of turmeric powder
¼ tsp of black seasame seeds
A pinch of salt
Sugar to taste
Coconut oil for frying

Method of preparation:

In a bowl mix flour, rice flour, sugar, turmeric powder, sesame seeds and salt by adding the required amount of water to make a batter of dropping consistency.

Cut the ripe plantains into thin slices.

Heat oil in a frying pan, dip the plantains in the batter and deep fry them out in oil till golden in colour and drain them on paper napkins.

Unnakkayi
Plantain rolls

Ingredients

4 Medium ripe plantains
Ghee for frying

For the filling
4 eggs
2 tbsps of Ghee
½ cup of sugar
3 tbsp of cashews
3 tbsp of raisins
Seeds of 3 cardamoms separated and crushed
¼ cup of scraped coconut

Method of preparation:

Steam the plantains and grind them into paste without adding water in a mixer bowl.

Beat the eggs and sugar together in a bowl.

In a pan pour ghee, fry and separate the cashews and raisins till they are golden in colour. Pour in the egg mixture, add in the coconut and scramble well. Add raisins, cashews and cardamoms to the mix and turn off the flame.

Grease both palms of your hands with ghee and make out small balls of plantain paste and flatten them into discs. Spoon the mixture in to the centre of the disc, lightly rolling it into the shape of a rugby ball.

In a pan pour ghee and when hot on medium flame slip the unnakkayis in to ghee. Turn both sides of the unnakkayi till they are uniformly golden in colour. This is a very famous Malabar snack.

Vattayappam
Steamed rice cake

Ingredients

¼ kg Raw rice
3 tbsps of cooked rice
1tsp of yeast granules dissolved in 1-2 tbsp of hot water
1tbsp sugar
Salt to taste

For grinding
½ cup scraped coconut
½ tsp cumin seeds
½ cup of shallots
2 cloves of garlic

For Vattayappam batter
1½ cup of sugar
½ cup of raisins

Method of preparation:

Wash and soak the raw rice for 4-5 hrs in water.
Once soaked, add cooked rice with it and grind it into a smooth paste by adding water and keep aside.

In a saucepan pour ¼ of the batter and 2 cups of plain water. Stir and cook the mixture on medium heat to make porridge.

Let the porridge cool down a bit and mix in the yeast. Now mix this to the rice batter thoroughly, cover and keep it overnight for fermentation.

Once the batter has been fermented, grind coconut, cumin, shallots & garlic to make a fine paste. Mix the paste with salt and sugar into the batter and keep it for about 20 minutes.

Grease plates with ghee , pour batter into the plates and steam it for about 15 minutes or until its done.

The raisins are to be added in between, then the batter is half set during steaming. so that the raisins stay on the top of the vattayappams.

Let it cool down and them cut them into cake slices.

Kinnathappam
Steamed jaggery rice cake

Ingredients

2 cups of rice flour
100g of Bengal gram dal (coarsely powdered)
2 cups of Jaggery syrup
3 cups of Coconut milk
3 Cardamoms, crushed
2 tbsp of Cashews (optional)
Ghee for greasing

Method of preparation:

Mix the rice flour, powdered gram dal, jaggery syrup, coconut milk and cardamom to make a loosened batter.

Keep the batter on low flame and stir with a ladle avoiding the formation of lumps. Pour 1tsp of ghee in between stirring.
When the batter starts getting thick, remove from flame.

In a ghee greased plate, pour the batter and steam it till a skewer comes out clean.

Kozhiada
Chicken pancakes

Ingredients

¼ kg of chicken pieces (boneless)
½ tsp of turmeric powder
5 green chillies
1 small piece of ginger, finely chopped
3 cloves of garlic, finely chopped
1 tsp of garam masala powder
1 tsp of vinegar
3 large onions, chopped
2 tbsp of oil
Salt to taste
Oil for frying
Curry leaves

For the crust

2 cups of all-purpose flour
50 ml of ghee
Salt to taste

Method of preparation:

Pressure-cook the chicken with turmeric powder and salt to taste.

Once cooked, when slightly cool, shred the chicken pieces in a food processor.

In a wok, heat oil, fry ginger, garlic, curry leaves and green chillies.
Then sauté in the onions till translucent.

Add the shredded chicken, stir adding garam masala to it. Remove from flame.

Make dough with the all-purpose flour adding salt and ghee along with water. Make about 25 balls out of the dough.

Roll out the balls to make thin discs. Place the required amount of chicken filling in the centre of the disc and fold it as a semicircle. Curl or flute the ends of the semicircle so that the filling is sealed.

Heat oil for frying and deep fry both sides of the kozhiada till golden in colour on medium flame.

This is a very popular Malabar Snack.

Kozhukatta

Steamed rice balls with coconut filling

Ingredients

For the dough

2 cups of rice flour
1 tsp of coconut oil
Salt to taste

For the filling

1 cup of scraped coconut
3/4 cup of Jaggery syrup
¼ tsp of cumin seeds
¼ tsp of dry ginger powder/ ¼ tsp of cardamom powder
1 tbsp of ghee

Method of preparation:

Boil water with the required amount of salt and add coconut oil. On medium flame stirring with the back part of a ladle, add in the rice flour till it comes together into soft dough. Turn off the flame and let it cool.

Once cool, knead the dough well with your hands, make medium sized balls and set aside. In a small wok, heat ghee fry the coconut along with cumin seeds and melted jaggery . Roast them well and add the cardamom powder.

Make depressions in the balls to form cups, spoon in the coconut balls and seal balls with your fingers.

Steam the kozhukattas till they are done or for 15 minutes on medium flame.

Inji curry
Ginger curry

Ingredients

1 large piece of ginger, finely chopped
3 green chillies, chopped
3 cloves of garlic chopped
A small gooseberry sized ball of tamarind
A small piece of Jaggery
½ tsp mustard seeds
1tbsp of oil
Curry leaves
Salt to taste

For frying
1 tsp of oil
100g coriander seeds
A pinch of aniseed
A pinch of raw rice
¼ tsp of fenugreek seeds
6 dry red chillies

Method of preparation:

In a pan pour oil and fry the items on medium flame for 5-10 minutes. Powder the fried ingredients in a mixer bowl and keep this aside.

In pan pour oil, pop mustard seeds, sauté ginger, greenchillies and garlic and pour tamarind water. When it starts simmering, add the coarsely powdered mix along with salt and stir.

Let the sauce thicken lightly and add a piece of jaggery and let it melt into the sauce.

Inji curry is one among the important items in a typical Kerala Sadhya. It is also known as Pulinji in some parts of Kerala.

It is best served with rice.

Irumbanpuli achar
Bilimbi Pickle

Ingredients

1kg of bilimbis
2 tsps of mustard seeds
1 1/2 tsp of split black lentils
1/2 tsp fenugreek seeds
1tsp turmeric powder
4 tbsps of kashmiri chilli powder
1/4 tsp Asafoetida powder
3/4 cup of gingelly oil
salt to taste
curry leaves

Method of preparation:

Slice the bilimbis into four lengthwise pieces and marinate them with salt. Keep it overnight and the next day; keep them in sunlight for about 4-5 hours.

Slightly roast the fenugreek seeds and urad dal and ground them into fine powder. In a wok heat the gingelly oil and splutter the mustard seeds.

Now turn off the flame and after a minute add in the powdered mix, asafoetida powder ,turmeric powder, kashmiri chilli powder while stirring . Now add in the salted bilimbis and mix well till they are well blended with the masala. Add in the curry leaves.

When it has cooled transfer them into clean and dry bottles. You can start using them within two days. In case after a week you feel the pickle is less spicy,heat about 2 tbsp of gingelly oil and add a tsp or two of chilli powder and pour it over the pickle and mix well.

Paal ada prathaman
Milk Pudding with rice flakes

Ingredients

200g of rice flakes/rice ada
500g of sugar
1 ½ litre milk
5-6 cardamoms, crushed
2 tbsp of Cashew nuts
2 tbsp of Raisins
50 ml ghee

Method of preparation:

Soak the rice flakes for 15 minutes in boiled water, covered with a lid.

In a thick bottomed vessel on medium flame, pour ghee and stir the rice flakes in it. Add milk and let the rice flakes cook, stirring the mix so that it doesn't stick to the bottom.

Once the rice flakes are soft and cooked, add sugar and cardamom and continue stirring.

When it starts getting thick remove from flame.

Fry cashews and raisins in 1 tbsp of ghee till golden in color and add to the payasam.

Paal ada prathaman is a dessert that can be served hot or cold.

Ada Prathaman
Jaggery rice pudding in coconut milk

Ingredients

200 g of rice flakes/rice ada
500g of jaggery made into syrup
4 cups of very thin coconut milk
2 cups of thin coconut milk
1 cup of thick coconut milk
6 cardamoms, slightly crushed
3 tbsp of cashews
3 tbsp of raisins
4 tbsp of ghee for frying cashews and raisins
50 ml of ghee

Method of preparation:

Wash the rice flakes and then soak it for 15 minutes in boiled water, covered with a lid. If the ada is not soft after 15 minutes cook it separately till soft and strain out the water.

In a flat bottomed heavy vessel onflame, pour ghee fry the cooked rice flakes for a few seconds and pour in the jaggery syrup. Stir till it thickens and add in the very thin coconut milk and continue stirring.

When the very thin milk is thickened, pour in the thin coconut milk with the crushed cardamoms and continue stirring.

Stir in the thick coconut milk and when it starts to simmer, remove from flame.

Fry cashews and raisins in ghee till golden in colour and mix in with the payasam.

Ada prathaman is a dessert that is best served with small bananas or pappadams.

Thulsi wine
Holy Basil wine

Ingredients

2 cups of thulsi leaves
Sugar
Water
1 tsp yeast

Method of preparation:

Wash the thulsi leaves well and put them into a bowl. Pour water into the bowl till you find the leaves floating.

Note the level of water in the bowl as that will be the measurement for sugar.

Pour the thulsi leaves with water into a saucepan and let it boil well till the water changes in colour.

Now let it cool down completely. Take a dry clean porcelain jar or bharani and measure in the sugar. When the thulsi concoction is well cooled pour it into the bharani and stir with a ladle so that the sugar and thulsi gets mixed.

Now add in a teaspoon of yeast to this and close the bharani tightly with a lid and store it in a dark place.

The wine will be fermented within 7 days. Please make sure to stir the thulsi mix once every day in clockwise direction with a ladle.

On the 7 th day seive out the thulasi wine through a muslin cloth. Store the wine in glass bottles.

The wine will be sweeter than the normal wines because if you cut down the sweetness the wine might slightly numb your tongue.

Tips to spring out the keralan touch in your cooking....

- Metric cups:
    - 1 cup…………………..250ml
    - ½ cup…………………..125ml
    - 1/3 cup………………….80ml
    - ¼ cup…………………..60ml
    - 1/8 cup………………….30ml
- Metric spoons:
    - 1tbsp……………20ml (about 4tsps)
    - 2tsps……………10ml
    - 1tsp………………5 ml
    - ½ tsp……………2.5ml
    - ¼ tsp…………..1.25ml

- Always try to use fresh curry leaves…that's the best thing to give your dish that extra zing.
- The Kashmiri chilli powder is less spicier than normal chilli powder.
- If you want to give that typical Keralan taste to your food, Iwould highly recommend you to use only and only … Coconut oil. You can use refined oil too but its best that you use coconut oil.
- Feel free to write in your queries and comments to me at nimi@nimisrecipes.com

With cups n cups of Cookin' love….

Nimi Sunilkumar

Notes